WITHDRAWN
UTSA LIBRARIES

1+641542
5-37

COLOMBIA: ARMED FORCES AND SOCIETY

by

J. Mark Ruhl

Foreign and Comparative Studies/Latin American Series I

Maxwell School of Citizenship and Public Affairs
Syracuse University
1980

Copyright

1980

by

MAXWELL SCHOOL OF CITIZENSHIP AND PUBLIC AFFAIRS

SYRACUSE UNIVERSITY, SYRACUSE, NEW YORK, U.S.A.

LIBRARY
The University of Texas
at San Antonio

Library of Congress Cataloging in Publication Data

Ruhl, J   Mark, 1948–
    Colombia.

    (Foreign and comparative studies : Latin American
series ; 1)
    Bibliography: p.
    1. Colombia--Armed Forces--Political activity.
2. Sociology, Military--Colombia. I. Title.
II. Series.
UA625.R83   322'.5'09861   80-18762
ISBN 0-915984-92-X

LIBRARY
The University of Texas
At San Anton

CONTENTS

iv

Note on Author

J. Mark Ruhl (1948-   ) is Assistant Professor of Political
Science and Director of the Latin American Studies Program at
Dickinson College in Carlisle, Pennsylvania. Professor Ruhl,
recipient of a Shell Foundation Dissertation Fellowship, received
his Ph.D. in political science from Syracuse University in 1975.
His research deals with the political consequences of modernization
in Latin America with special emphasis on the Colombian case.
Recent articles by Professor Ruhl have appeared in <u>Latin American
Research Review</u>, <u>Inter-American Economic Affairs</u>, and in Albert
Berry et al., <u>Politics of Compromise: Coalition Government in
Colombia</u> (New Brunswick: Transaction Books, 1980).

INTRODUCTION[*]

Military government is the norm in Latin America. Moreover, during the past decade, the armed forces have assumed control not only in countries that have had long histories of military intervention but also in nations that have had strong traditions of civilian rule, e.g., Chile and Uruguay. Indeed, many contemporary juntas have taken power with the intention of retaining authority indefinitely in order to effect fundamental changes in their societies. Our knowledge of military behavior and ideology has been greatly enhanced by the literature that has described these new, more active, and institutionalized military regimes (See Lowenthal, 1976). Nevertheless, there is still much to be learned from a closer examination of civil-military relations in the few nations where civilian government has persisted. The purpose of this analysis is, therefore, to contribute to a better understanding of the Latin American military by attempting to describe and explain the Colombian military's deviation from the contemporary norm of intervention.

THEORETICAL PERSPECTIVES

Students of Latin American politics draw upon a number of general theorists in order to account for the high incidence of military government in the region. The most commonly used theoretical framework is provided by Huntington (1968) whose theory of political decay figures prominently in the works of such scholars as Stepan (1971, 1973, 1978), O'Donnell (1973, 1976, 1978), and Lowenthal (1976). Huntington (1968: 194) argues that

the most important causes of military intervention
in politics are not military but political and reflect

[*]The author wishes to thank Robert Nilsson, Gene Rosi Fred Woerner, Harry Dull, Ron McDonald, Shirley Hall, and Penny Homolash for their assistance and to acknowledge the support of the Dickinson College Research and Development Fund.

> not the social and organizational characteristics
> of the military establishment but the political
> and institutional structure of the society.

Huntington's analysis begins with the concept of social mobilization which is defined as the process by which traditional social,
economic and psychological commitments are eroded by modernization,
thus making people available for more modern patterns of social and
political behavior (1968: 33). Specifically, he suggests that as
a nation becomes more highly socially mobilized, e.g., more literate and more urban, societal demands for greater material well-being
and social equality will increase significantly. Under these circumstances political order becomes much more difficult to maintain.
Indeed, unless these new societal demands are satisfied or civilian
political institutions become strong enough to manage them, a condition of political decay indicated by political violence, failing
civilian regimes, and military intervention will result. Huntington refers to such societies as "praetorian" since, although all
social forces become politicized and compete with one another directly in the absence of adequate institutional buffers, the armed
forces generally dominate because of their greater command of the
tools of violence.

Many analysts suggest, therefore, that military government
is common in contemporary Latin America because most of the countries in the area have become praetorian societies. Latin American social mobilization levels have risen markedly in recent decades
while efforts to broaden the distribution of economic benefits or
to construct strong civilian political institutions have been generally unsuccessful. Consequently, most Latin American nations are
characterized by political decay and civilian governmental collapse.
O'Donnell (1976: 203), for example, argues that Argentina's high
level of social mobilization coupled with economic stagnation and
civilian political failure created a situation of mass praetorianism
in which military intervention became a frequent occurrence.
Stepan's (1971) classic study of Brazilian civil-military relations
also links military intervention to the praetorian condition. With
ample reference to Huntington, Stepan carefully documents a prae-

torian pattern of rising social mobilization, a stalled economy, and weak, fractionalized political institutions that precipitated the military coup of 1964. Many other scholars also draw upon Huntington's theory and the praetorian concept. McDonald (1975), for example, uses the model to explain the Uruguayan military's takeover of governmental power during the early 1970's. Praetorian conditions and military coups have, of course, long been common in Latin America even at relatively modest levels of social mobilization; however, conditions of political decay have only recently begun to lead to the institutionalized military regimes that currently rule in Brazil, Chile, Uruguay, and Argentina.[1] Both O'Donnell and Stepan have sought to elaborate upon Huntington's basic framework in order to explain the rise of this new type of Latin American military regime.

O'Donnell (1973, 1976) suggests that the more active, institutionalized military government most probably arises in a praetorian society where civilian political failure coexists with a high level of modernization, i.e., high social mobilization and economic complexity. In these societies, the organized urban popular sector created or "mobilized" by industrialization commonly threatens the traditional civilian elite's ability to retain political control. In contemporary Latin America, this difficult political situation is linked to an economic crisis since nearly all of the more complex economies are now faced with a critical need for economic austerity and massive new investment because of the exhaustion of the easy phases of import substitution industrialization that most experienced from the early 1930's to the mid-1950's. The mobilized popular sector, however, has become strong enough to resist the civilian elite's demands for economic sacrifices and to frighten away needed foreign investment. The economy, therefore, lacks the necessary burst of new investment to restart economic growth and thus continues to stagnate. Moreover, the common indicators of this economic crisis, such as rising inflation, falling investment, and declining GNP growth, further undermine civilian government cohesion and legitimacy and exacerbate the political crisis.

Under these unstable conditions, the armed forces initially
suffer severe internal political fractionalization as many different military factions participate directly in the mobilized political arena acting as allies of various civilian sectors; however,
this fractionalization within the military organization

> implies great costs for the military officers
> in terms of threats to the survival of their
> organization, uncertainty in their personal careers
> and the severe reduction of their possibilities of
> power over the national political processes
> (O'Donnell, 1976: 220).

In time, the military officers begin to realize that they share a
common corporate interest in a temporary exit from this chaotic
political activity and in a concentration on military professionalization; instability actually encourages increased professionalization.

Yet, as the military becomes increasingly professionalized,
i.e., better organized, educated, and technically sophisticated,
its internal cohesion also grows as does its sense of institutional
superiority, vis-à-vis the chronic failure of civilian governments
to manage the economic and political crisis. In addition, the
persistence of praetorian conditions and particularly the threat
of the urban Left are eventually seen to endanger the professional
military's new cohesion and perhaps its very existence. Thus,
when the military enters politics again, it enters as a unified
institution intent on a major transformation of society that will
end the praetorian conditions. O'Donnell (1976: 230) notes that

> this coup d'état implies a level of political participa-
> tion by the military and a militarization of social
> problems which greatly exceed what could have been
> attempted by officers of a less professionalized insti-
> tution. Therefore in conditions of high modernization,
> a relatively high level of military professionalization
> is achieved which in short order induces the most intense
> and comprehensive type of military politicization.

O'Donnell argues that this process explains both the professionalization drives of the Argentine and Brazilian militaries in the
early 1960's and their consequent creation of "bureaucratic-authoritarian" regimes. In Brazil after the 1964 coup and in Argentina
after the 1966 and 1976 coups, the military sought to suppress

social conflict, exclude dissenting political groups, and institute
a military-directed, technocratic model of economic development
which entailed both austerity and the attempted attraction of
massive new foreign investment. These were the professional militaries' solutions to the problems posed by social mobilization and
economic development in Latin America.

These developments totally contradicted traditional theories
which linked increased military professionalism to obedient apolitical military behavior toward civilian authority as described in
Huntington's early work, The Soldier and the State (1957). While
O'Donnell has explained this contradiction in terms of the severe
economic and political crises described above, Stepan (1973) has
placed greater emphasis on the effects of perceived threats of
guerrilla warfare and revolution on professional military thinking.
Essentially, Stepan (1973: 47-65) has linked the rise of the "New
Professionalism" of the Latin American military and the creation
of the institutionalized army governments to the counterinsurgency
doctrines exported by the United States during the early 1960's.
The Cuban Revolution's success and the prevalence of other guerrilla movements in Latin America during this period stimulated many
military institutions, especially the more professionalized ones,
to define their mission largely in terms of maintaining internal
security. Stepan (1973: 50-51) notes that

> the formulators of United States military assistance
> programs and the chiefs of many Latin American military
> establishments now believed that professional military
> expertise was required in a broader range of fields...
> hence the military institutions began to study such
> questions as the social and political conditions facil-
> itating the growth of revolutionary protest.

When this attempt by the armed forces to analyze and devise solutions for a broad range of national problems took place in a context of weak civilian legitimacy and political decay, the military's concept of its institutional role tended to expand considerably. The military in Brazil and Peru, for instance, saw national security seriously endangered by a host of social and economic
problems which civilian politicians had been unable or unwilling
to solve. The professional armed forces could not afford to be

apolitical in these circumstances. Indeed, the only solution seemed to be an extended era of major societal change carried out by the professional military itself.

Once in power, the Peruvian military, of course, acted rather differently from the Brazilian military. Many reasons have been offered by Stepan (1973: 62-64) and others (Einaudi, 1973: 71-87) to account for this dissimilarity but the most convincing ones have explained the contrasts between the two military regimes by reference to differences in the modernization levels of Brazil and Peru. In more modernized Brazil, worker and peasant organizations were more highly developed and already were demanding radical changes in society. From the military's perspective, these groups and the populist political class constituted the most immediate threats to national security, development, and the military institution. Thus such groups had to be politically excluded and coerced into accepting orthodox economic policies. In less modernized Peru, lower class organizations were smaller and less radical. Neither they nor the weak Peruvian guerrilla movement that was defeated in 1966 really posed any threat to political order or the armed forces. The Peruvian officers, therefore, began to perceive the undynamic and corrupt civilian elite as the principal obstacle to national development. Hence, according to Stepan's (1973: 64) analysis

> in Peru the military government has been largely
> concerned with nationalism and development and this
> has meant that significant opposition from the Left
> is absent.

This pattern characterized Peruvian politics until the mid-1970's when economic collapse and growing political mobilization led the military to adopt more conservative policies.

It becomes clear from this brief discussion that military intervention will be most probable under praetorian conditions in which civilian political institutions become overburdened because of the pressures of social and economic change. Moreover, if such conditions occur in more modernized nations where the military has become highly professionalized and perhaps is also influenced by modern counterinsurgency doctrines, military intervention will probably result in the creation of a highly active, institutionalized military government. Thus, in order to understand why Colombia has retained civilian government and has not yet experienced this type of bureaucratic-authoritarian military regime, two factors must be examined: the nature of Colombian society and the professional experience of the Colombian armed forces. The following analysis will argue 1) that Colombia's pattern of civil-military relations is an atypical one because Colombia, unlike most Latin American nations, has not yet become a politically unstable praetorian society and 2) that, therefore, although the Colombian military has become stronger and more professionalized in recent years in contrast to its historical weakness, the competence and legitimacy of Colombia's civilian political elite has inhibited the development of unified armed forces support for alternative military solutions to the nation's problems. The following section of the paper briefly examines contemporary Colombian society, economy, and politics in order to evaluate the degree to which Colombia deviates from the praetorian characteristics that Huntington, O'Donnell, and Stepan associate with military intervention. The development and behavior of the armed forces will then be discussed at length.

SOCIAL AND ECONOMIC CHANGE IN COLOMBIA

A number of scholars including Leal Buitrago (1973) and Campos-McCamant (1972) have designated Colombia as a modernizing society ripe for every manner of major political disorder from military coup to social revolution. Indeed, many commonly used quantitative indicators suggest that Colombia has begun to approach a potentially dangerous level of social mobilization. Three-quarters of the adult population is literate and over two-thirds of the nation lives in cities (Wiarda and Kline, 1979: 5). Colombia is now Latin America's fifth most urban nation (See Appendix A for comparative data). Such statistics coupled with other figures that document the expansion of mass communication and transportation networks are generally used to indicate the erosion of

traditional passive peasant society and the rise of a more aware
and potentially demanding population that Huntington has linked to
political instability.

A number of qualifying observations need to be introduced to
modify this misleading perspective. First, compared to the rest
of Latin America, Colombia's rate of social mobilization has been
especially rapid particularly with respect to urbanization. In
1951 only 39% of the population lived in cities, therefore, a great
number of urban dwellers in comtemporary Colombia must still be
first generation migrants (Schoultz, 1972). Empirical research by
Mangin (1967), Peattie (1972) and others has shown that new migrants
are less frustrated and demanding than the general urban population;
studies of Bogotá's slum barrios by Van Es and Flinn (1973) con-
firm these findings for Colombia's largest city. The new migrant
may feel that he has improved his status and opportunities simply
by entering the more sophisticated, hopeful, urban environment where
his access to public services is much improved. The former peasant also tends to retain his traditional rural social deference
and is relatively uninterested in joining active political groups.
Furthermore, recent research by Cornelius (1974) and Handelman
(1975) demonstrates that most members of the second and later
generations of the urban poor may remain politically passive as
long as they lack regular employment as industrial workers particularly if anti-system political movements seem too weak to pose a
serious threat to the existing government. As members of the urban
marginal class sporadically employed in the unstable service sector,
e.g., domestic servants and street vendors, such individuals are
forced to devote most of their energies to daily survival and cannot afford to risk support for political causes that appear to be
stillborn.

For these reasons, it appears that Colombia's social mobilization level, as indicated by the high percentage of the population
living in urban areas, has been consistently inflated by the unusually high number of new migrants and the marginally employed that it
encompasses. Many of the children of the 1950-1980 migrants have
not yet come of political age and the lack of urban industrial

employment in Colombia, due in part to its capital-intensive industrial sector, has further inhibited the politicization of second
generation urban dwellers. By modernizing later than many Latin
American industrial sectors, Colombian industry has been able to
make use of the most technologically sophisticated modes of production which require far fewer workers. In this urban environment
of chronic unemployment, labor unions tend to be relatively small
and co-optable. Thus, although Colombia's urban population is large
and outbreaks of urban violence do occur, the nation's urban centers do not pose the mobilized threat to the system that is represented by the older and better organized urban concentrations of
Argentina, Chile or Uruguay. In each of these three nations, the
most rapid urbanization phase took place decades ago when urban
industrial employment opportunities were greater because of the
earlier, less automated type of industrial technology. Strong
union organizations and, in some cases, durable political parties
based in the working class, e.g., Argentine Peronists, grew out of
the large industrial proletariats and have never been politically
absorbed. No such movements as these have succeeded in Colombia.

Rural Colombia also has not become as socially mobilized as
its rising literacy level and declining isolation might imply.
The "demobilizing" effect of La Violencia (1946-1957) may be the
most important factor contributing to the surprisingly low level
of rural demands. Weinert (1966), Fals Borda (1965), and others
suggest that this brutal experience of inter-party conflict which
cost over 200,000 lives accelerated the breakdown of traditional
rural society. Nevertheless, although peasants may no longer be
as firmly controlled by traditional authority structures, they may
not yet be ready for political action because of their fears of
further violence. Huntington (1968: 327) cites post-civil war
Spain and Mexico as examples to show that

> sustained violence produces physical, human, and moral
> exhaustion which eventually leads a society to accept
> any sort of order.

Dix (1967: 382) notes that studies of refugees from La Violencia
revealed a widespread condition of confusion and valuelessness.
An important peasant organization, the Asociación Nacional de

Usuarios Campesinos (ANUC), was formed in 1967 and some of its members have begun to demand more radical changes in Colombia's inequitable land tenure system. Nonetheless, the historical experience of La Violencia seems to keep rural Colombia a less politically active and a less potentially threatening area than one might expect, given the impact of socially mobilizing forces. No other Latin American nation has experienced such profound rural violence as recently as Colombia.

In short, this analysis suggests that Colombia's actual level of social mobilization is substantially lower than that indicated by standard quantitative measures, given 1) the high percentage of urban dwellers who are either new migrants and/or economically marginal and 2) the traumatic rural experience of La Violencia. Consequently, although Colombia is much more socially mobilized than it was thirty years ago, mass demands are apparently lower and more manageable than many scholars have suggested. Therefore, the praetorian condition associated with high social mobilization may still be avoidable.

Pressures on the civilian elite have been increasing, however, because the Colombian economy with a GDP of $795 per capita (Colombia Today, 1979) has not yet been able to satisfy very many of the mass expectations that modernization has generated; Colombia suffers from the common structural problems that plague most Latin American economies. For instance, although domestic industry has expanded in recent years, Colombia is still dependent on its agricultural sector and particularly on the success of its coffee exports. Coffee has traditionally provided at least 70% of total export earnings. This level was reduced to about 50% during the 1973-1975 period through export diversification but the performance of the Colombian economy remains precariously bound to fluctuating world coffee demand. The 1975-1977 boom in world prices caused by temporary shortages of exportable coffee in Brazil, Angola, and elsewhere, obviously benefited Colombia despite the difficult inflationary side-effects it caused; however, this windfall began to erode in 1978 as world production began to return to more normal levels. Coffee sales are especially important to the performance of the

Colombian economy and a price fall, therefore, is more serious because the rest of the agricultural sector is particularly inefficient and unproductive. The large landowners who control most of Colombia's non-coffee agricultural production are notorious for their failure to invest enough capital to raise agricultural production substantially. Today, the domestic agricultural sector still cannot fulfill Colombia's basic food requirements.

The industrial sector also confronts fundamental problems. Colombia has industrialized to its present modest level (19.2% of the GNP is in manufacturing) largely by manufacturing consumer goods that previously were imported (Wiarda and Kline, 1979: 5). This standard import substitution strategy has now reached a saturation point. With fewer imported consumer goods remaining to be substituted (9% of 1978 imports), Colombia is attempting the extremely costly and much more difficult step of developing an intermediate and capital goods industry (Colombia Today, 1979). In order to gradually expand industry in this fashion, Colombia must acquire considerable export earnings as well as substantial foreign investment. Domestic private sources of investment have never been sufficient while public investment has been hindered by the government's traditionally weak revenue foundation; taxes are still too closely related to export success. Thus, when coffee and other export earnings are low and foreign investment scarce, Colombian industry stagnates. Unfortunately, these two conditions often coincide because investment is customarily most attracted to the country when successful exports stimulate or are expected to stimulate general economic performance. Moreover, under the most favorable conditions, the growth of Colombian industry is still limited by the fact that current markets are too small to absorb greatly increased production. Low wages and poor income distribution restrict the domestic market and foreign markets are only beginning to open up to Colombian industrial goods.

Depending on coffee exports and characterized by inefficient agriculture and semi-developed industry, the growth of the Colombian economy has been inconsistent and marked by double-digit inflation. Since 1968, GDP growth rates have been more

promising than usual averaging over 6% per year due to strong
legitimate and clandestine (drug-related) export earnings and improved government planning; however, the rapid population growth
rate of approximately 2.5% per year has diminished the positive
effects of this recent improvement. In addition, the modest economic growth benefits that remain have not been shared equally.
Distribution of income, like distribution of land in Colombia, is
highly inequitable. The top 20% of the population earns more than
60% of the total income while under 5% of land holdings encompass
over 65% of arable land despite a small agrarian reform program
(Urrutia and Berry, 1975). The majority of Colombians, including
those who have been socially mobilized, remain underemployed, des-
perately poor, and undernourished whether they live in the cities
or in the countryside. The Colombian economic situation is typical
of many Latin American nations. In fact, mass economic benefits
are so minimal that Colombia's adjusted moderate level of social
mobilization might have caused praetorian conditions had it not
been for the nation's strong civilian political institutions.

COLOMBIAN GOVERNMENT AND POLITICS

The key to Colombia's stable civil-military relations lies in
the present effectiveness and legitimacy of traditional political
party leadership. The multi-class Liberal and Conservative parties
still dominate Colombian political life although the fierce inter-
party rivalry that characterized Colombia's 19th century history
and later led to La Violencia (1945-1957) no longer exists. Fright-
ened by the future potential for class violence that La Violencia
suggested and having experienced a brief and unpleasant period of
military dictatorship under populist General Gustavo Rojas Pinilla
(1953-1957), to be described below, the nation's social elite de-
cided to bury past partisan differences (Wilde, 1978). Under the
National Front agreement, the two parties agreed to divide legis-
lative and bureaucratic positions equally and to alternate the
Presidency every four years from 1958 to 1974. This form of
coalition government has proven to be a successful means of

elite compromise. During this period, the Conservative and Liberal party leaders demonstrated a growing ability to cooperate in
support of a joint program of pragmatic, defensive reform that was
designed to keep them securely in power.

The National Front governments gradually increased the elite's
ability to manage economic development and institute moderate social reforms. The Colombian bureaucracy was enlarged and professionalized particularly through the development of new decentral-
ized agencies (Bailey, 1977). Of the twenty-five institutions
most directly involved in economic planning, for instance, nine-
teen were National Front creations (Garces, 1972:147). Government
expenditures in real pesos per capita rose 137% between 1959 and
1970 reflecting the broader scope of governmental activity
(Villegas, 1972: 174-175). The greatest increase in governmental
action took place after the 1966 election of Liberal President
Carlos Lleras Restrepo who, by means of new taxes and better tax
administration, greatly improved the government's financial base.
Lleras was also responsible for greatly stimulating Colombian
non-traditional exports by adopting a more flexible exchange rate
and by dismantling protective trade barriers that had become coun-
terproductive despite strong domestic opposition (Berry, 1980:
301-304). It should be noted that United States' aid also helped
the National Front administrations especially between 1960 and
1967 when American assistance equaled 1.9% of the GDP and allowed
approximately a 50% increase in governmental investment (Campos-
McCamant, 1972:25-26). Individual National Front regimes varied
in their abilities to direct Colombia's difficult economy but the
era as a whole showed a marked improvement in governmental performance. Some moderate social reforms such as increased educational
expenditures and a small agrarian reform were also implemented by
the National Front. Under the National Front the civilian political elite increased its ability to deal with the nation's economic
and social problems although the effects of elite efforts have not
yet resulted in a substantially improved level of material well-
being for most Colombians.

The first two post-National Front governments, that of

Liberal Alfonso López Michelsen (1974–1978) and that of his
successor Julio César Turbay Ayala (1978–1982), have continued to
govern in this tradition of pragmatic reform and careful economic
management. For example, when faced with rising inflation (30%)
and a large deficit upon taking office, López instituted a harsh
economic austerity program after declaring a state of economic
emergency in September 1974. His stabilization program entailed
wage restrictions, fiscal controls, and reduced governmental sub-
sidies which initially resulted in unemployment, falling industrial activity, and considerable popular opposition. In fact, the
additional inflationary stress caused by the coffee bonanza forced
López to maintain these unpopular policies throughout his entire
term (Gómez Buendía, 1978). The violent general strike of September 1977 suggested some of the unrest those conservative policies
generated. Nevertheless, by 1978, the positive longer-term effects
of López's austerity program were evident to most observers as the
Turbay government inherited a falling inflation rate, steady economic growth, and a very favorable foreign reserve position. Careful, relatively orthodox economic policies have been continued under Turbay.

Although López chose a distinctly non-populist response to
Colombia's economic problems, he also pursued a variety of more
broadly popular reform measures. His tax reform increased governmental revenues by drawing more heavily on the wealthier classes;
he also expanded educational opportunities in Colombia at the expense of the private schools. Moreover, López maintained a popular, rather nationalistic, foreign policy by recognizing Cuba,
supporting Panama on the canal issue, and forcing previously for-
eign-owned banks to become 51% Colombian-owned. Turbay's opposition to Nicaragua's Somoza before the dictator's downfall in 1979
can be viewed as part of the same pattern. López and Turbay have
traveled this cautious path between conservative economic policy
and more reformist social and foreign policies with the support
of much of the Conservative Party, members of which have held seats
in their cabinets. The traditional parties have maintained their
consensus on pragmatic defensive reform and have continued the

principle of minority cabinet and administrative representation.
Although both parties suffer innumerable factional divisions, the
in-fighting has not been serious enough to threaten the general
agreement on basic principles.

Despite the fact that some of the civilian political elite's
policies have been unpopular, especially during periods of economic stress, the level of mass support for the traditional parties
has remained rather high. In the pre-National Front years, the
two traditional patron-client parties could take widespread mass
support for granted because of the tradition of hereditary party
identification. Party loyalties growing out of the armed and electoral conflicts of the 19th century have been stronger and more
broadly held in Colombia than anywhere else in Latin America
(Bushnel, 1971). Yet, although in the 20th century party identification still retained a near religious quality, the elite's mass
support base seemed in doubt during the latter part of the National
Front. Initially, the civilian politicians worried because electoral abstentions began to grow (73% in 1968) but this problem was
attributed to the fact that elections under the parity arrangement
had become uninteresting contests between organized factions within each of the two traditional parties. A more serious danger
presented itself when populist former General Gustavo Rojas organized the ideologically amorphous Alianza Nacional Popular (ANAPO)
to oppose the National Front and began to run ANAPO in both Conservative and Liberal races. In April 1970, lower class based
ANAPO reached its peak by gaining almost 36% of the Congressional
vote and nearly electing Rojas, who ran as a nominal Conservative,
to the Presidency.

At the time, a great deal of concern was expressed about this
apparent ANAPO threat to the traditional elite and to the pattern
of hereditary party identification that helped the elite remain
in power. However, between 1970 and 1974, the ANAPO movement
nearly disintegrated and mass support for the traditional political parties returned to pre-ANAPO levels. In the 1972 department-
al elections, when ANAPO first ran as an independent party, its
support fell to under 19% of the vote. In 1974, after adopting

a more clearly Leftist political platform under the leadership of Rojas' daughter María Eugenia Rojas, the party declined further (Dix, 1978: 348). About half of the ANAPO Congressmen returned to the traditional parties from which they had come and María Eugenia Rojas captured under 10% of the presidential vote, considerably less than either of the traditional party candidates, Liberal Alfonso López Michelsen (56%) and Conservative Álvaro Gómez Hurtado (32%). In the 1978 election, the traditional parties' share of the total vote actually increased to 96% as Turbay won a narrow victory over Conservative Belisario Betancur. Neither ANAPO nor the small, factionalized Marxist opposition was able to generate more than token support (Ruhl, 1978; Hoskin, 1979).

In short, although the Colombian civilian political elite's traditionally high level of mass support seemed threatened by ANAPO, it actually survived the National Front era more or less intact. When normal inter-party competition was restored in 1974 and ANAPO ran as a clearly independent, anti-system party, most of its voters returned to the traditional parties which they had, in a sense, never left because before 1972, voters had cast ANAPO ballots under one of the traditional party labels. Although abstention was rather high (59%) again in 1978 reflecting, at least in part, some weakening of traditional party loyalties, those who voted again overwhelmingly chose to case their ballots for the Conservative or Liberal parties.

This analysis suggests that the National Front arrangements helped measurably to increase the strength of Colombian civilian political institutions. The civilian political elite became more cohesive and improved its governmental capacity to deal with the economic and social problems of modernization. The elite was also able to retain the rather high level of mass support for the traditional political parties without resorting to the populist economic policies that would have damaged Colombia's economic future and invited military concern. The relative legitimacy of the Colombian political system is becoming clear even to those who regret the civilian elite's selfish, and admittedly limited, conception of socioeconomic reform. As Peeler (1976: 223) observes, the

> Colombian party system, though indeed corrupt by
> widely accepted value standards, is objectively
> viable and will remain broadly stable in the fore-
> seeable future. Justice is not a precondition for
> the survival of political order.

Neither Colombia's small Marxist guerrilla movements nor the regular outbreaks of violent strikes or demonstrations seems significant beside this picture of underlying political order. Colombia's
rising social mobilization and structural economic deficiencies
may, in the future, lead to the type of praetorian politics that
characterize much of Latin America; however, currently, civilian
political institutions are capable and legitimate enough to maintain political order and to avoid the praetorian syndrome that
Huntington, O'Donnell, and others have linked to military intervention. There is no sense of national economic crisis or political breakdown that would encourage the military to become an
alternative government.

COLOMBIAN MILITARY HISTORY

The traditional strength and effectiveness of the civilian
political elite has had a major historical impact on the development and professional status of the Colombian military. Although
the Colombian armed forces' obedience to civilian rule is rare for
contemporary Latin America, such a relationship is not irregular
from the perspective of Colombia's own history. Civilian control
of the military has been the norm since the early years of independence. The officer corps of Colombia's original independence army
was filled with the same creole aristocrats who formed the core
of the 19th century military castes of other Latin American nations.
Yet, this army and its officers were soon destroyed by the Spanish
and replaced by Bolívar's Venezuelan, predominantly lower class
forces (Maingot, 1969). The Colombian aristocracy and general
public found this new racially mixed army distasteful but necessary
in the war against Spain. After hostilities ceased, the civilian
politicians of Bogotá moved quickly to reduce the military's size
and influence. Later, when the Gran Colombia federation split in

1830, most of the Venezuelan officers left or were expelled from
the country. The Colombian political elite rejoiced. The military,
now under the direction of Colombian intellectual José María Obando,
was further reduced in size to under 2,500 men and placed securely
under the control of the Colombian Congress. The civilian elite
kept the army small in subsequent years and delegated to it only
insignificant tasks, e.g., mail delivery and supervision of leprosy
asylums (Maingot, 1970: 142). Few members of the Colombian aristocracy were attracted by such duties or by the low status institution that performed them. The unprofessional military played virtually no role in the active political life of this period.

Some years later, a dissident faction of Liberals, composed
mostly of lower class urban artisans, did enlist the support of
the small army then under the command of General José María Melo
and managed briefly to take control of Bogota in 1854. Nevertheless, this government had survived only about seven months when it
was ousted by a civilian coalition led by Liberal and Conservative
members of the aristocracy. After regaining power, the civilians
almost disbanded the national military, leaving only a few small
units for simple police and guard duty functions. Thus, Maingot
(1970: 145) notes that unlike other Latin American nations,
Colombia

> began its national political life at a time when the
> military institution was for all practical purposes
> nonexistent. The system of social sanctions and rewards,
> controlled by the civilians, kept the military sub-
> ordinate from then on.

Although Colombia experienced innumerable violent civil wars
during the rest of the 19th century, the tiny national army, its few
officers recruited from marginal classes, played no appreciable
role in these conflicts. The civil wars were largely waged by
amateur officer-politicans from the two political parties. In this
unstable and highly partisan climate, all attempts to build a regular professional army were frustrated until after the War of the
Thousand Days (1899-1902), the most violent of the party wars,
ushered in a long era of peace (Helguera, 1961). In short,
although 19th century Colombia certainly qualified as a violent,

praetorian society well before the era of massive socioeconomic change, there was no professional military institution to take advantage of the situation.

The creation of a professional armed forces began with the reforma militar of Conservative President Rafael Reyes (1904-1909). Reyes hoped to build a national army that would help to enforce the truce between the Liberals and Conservatives and he therefore invited a mission of German-trained Chilean officers to assist in the process of professionalization. In 1907, the Chileans helped found and staff a military academy, the Escuela Militar de Cadetes, and began a systematic program for officer recruitment. Many sons of the civilian elite were initially attracted to the school and were instructed in the latest European military theories and techniques.

Although three Chilean missions visited Colombia between 1907 and 1913 and founded the Escuela Superior de Guerra for advanced military studies, early enthusiasm for the new military career soon faded. Two-thirds of the military academy's early graduates did not enter the army (Maingot, 1970: 157). Other small, foreign military missions came to Colombia in later years, e.g., the Swiss (1924-1927), and continued to instruct the small 1,500 man army. Nevertheless, Colombian officers remained very inadequately trained in comparison to their Latin American counterparts. Few officers were drawn from socially prominent families and the Colombian military failed to develop a sense of institutional cohesion or corporate identity.

During this untroubled period of partisan compromise, the civilian elite was able to manage the initial social pressures of modernization without any fear that the weak professional army might interfere in politics. Yet the new military did prove to be a useful tool of the elite in controlling outbreaks of worker or peasant violence as in the infamous United Fruit Strike of 1928. The army also served between 1932 and 1934 in a limited frontier conflict with Peru near Leticia. Although few troops were involved in this confrontation, the action instilled some sense of mission in the armed forces and led to a modest expansion in size and in internal educational programs, e.g., Escuela de Infantería (1933) and Escuela de Caballería (1936); however, not long before the era of elite compromise ended, the Colombian army of about 6,000 men constituted one of Latin America's least important military forces.

During the early years of the 20th century, Colombia was an orderly country controlled by two effective and legitimate civilian political parties. This pattern was not to last. Between the mid-1930's and the mid-1950's, the party elites' compromise fractured and Colombia gradually returned to a style of praetorian politics reminiscent of the 19th century. Within the context of growing violence and political decay, the regular armed forces expanded, gained influence, and ultimately took control of government for the first time in a century.

This fundamental change in Colombian military behavior was set in motion by the electoral victory of Liberal President Alfonso López Pumarejo in 1934. Although predominantly Conservative in partisan orientation, the army had accepted the election of the first 20th century Liberal President Enrique Olaya Herrera in 1930. Olaya Herrera's successor López, however, with his strong support among the new urban and working classes was much more antagonistically partisan and viewed the small army as a potentially dangerous Conservative threat to his program of social reform. Rueda Vargas (1944: 259), an early student of the Colombian military, noted that the officer corps grew fearful that partisanship would interfere with military personnel and advancement policies under López. Mutual hostility between López and the officer corps mounted when the President, as expected, began to meddle with promotions and command assignments in order to favor Liberal officers. Moreover, Lopez created a Liberal national police force as a check on the regular armed forces while he tried to divert the regulars to the nonmilitary task of colonizing remote areas of the country. Under the Liberal regime, all soldiers were also disenfranchised and prohibited from joining political parties. Many officers were angry with these attempts to manipulate the armed forces and with López's condescending attitude toward the military profession. Dix (1967: 297) notes that the President often referred to the soldiers in public as "parasites." Perhaps the best indication of the officer corps' lack of cohesion and corporate identity is the fact that only one minor conspiracy to depose López surfaced in the military (1936) during his first term despite his repeated attacks on the armed forces.

López's successor, Eduardo Santos (1938-1942), was a more moderate Liberal, both with respect to social reforms and to civil-military relations. Consequently, partisan tension and military dissatisfaction subsided. The Santos government also showed concern for military professionalization. United States naval and air force missions visited Colombia at this time and the curriculum of the Escuela Militar was updated in 1942 (Maingot, 1970: 153). Alfonso López's re-election in the same year, however, led to a resumption of civil-military difficulties. The second López administration was characterized by a climate of growing social tensions, partisan crises, and public scandal. In this context of progressively deteriorating civilian politics and renewed civil-military frictions, a faction of the officer corps made a more serious attempt to oust López in 1944.

While López was attending the army's annual maneuvers near the Ecuadorian border, he was placed under arrest in Pasto by Colonel Diógenes Gil Mojica. Gil also imprisoned troops loyal to the President and issued a public appeal to the rest of the army and nation to join his anti-López revolt. Most officers were unhappy with López and Gil had about a quarter of the Colombian army with him in Pasto; thus, this attempt presented a serious threat to the government (Icenhour, 1976; Leal Buitrago, 1970). Unfortunately for Gil and his co-conspirators, the coup proved unsuccessful. In Bogotá, Vice-President Dario Echandía, who declared himself acting-President in this emergency, was able to appeal to the military's traditional sense of obedience to elected civilian authority. After the Minister of War, General Espinel Domingo and the Bogotá garrison declared their loyalty to the civilian government, the Pasto coup collapsed. Colonel Gil fled and other disloyal officers were arrested. Upon López's release, he promptly dismissed a number of Conservative officers, some of whom

apparently had little direct connection with the conspiracy.
Clearly, Colombian politics had moved closer to the praetorian
model although most officers as yet were unwilling to contemplate
military intervention.

Conservative Mariano Ospina Pérez was elected President in
1946 because a division in the majority party produced two Liberal
candidates. Although Ospina began his term with a coalition cabinet, rising inter-party conflict shortly made compromise impossible.
Rural violence between Liberal and Conservative partisans raged
out of control in some provinces as early as 1946. Military
officers were assigned to govern many of these troubled areas and,
hence, became directly embroiled in the inter-party conflict. The
army also came to the defense of Ospina Pérez during the urban mob
violence or Bogotazo that followed the assassination of Liberal
leader Jorge Eliécar Gaitán in April 1948. The national police,
who had deserted Ospina Pérez in this crisis, were placed under
direct army command. Later, when Liberals left the Cabinet in
protest against Conservative rural repression, they were replaced
by military officers. Ultimately, the armed forces cooperated
with the forced closing of the Liberal-controlled Congress and
with the unopposed election of Ospina's successor, Conservative
Laureano Gómez, in 1950.[2]

As La Violencia raged in rural Colombia, Gómez imposed an ever
more rigid Conservative dictatorship. The military defended the
Conservative regime against the Liberal guerrillas and was rewarded
by the government with institutional expansion; the military's share
of the Colombian budget rose from 15.7% in 1950 to 22.5% in 1953
(Maullin, 1973: 83). In addition, the Conservative politicians
handled the armed forces with great respect and deference. High
ranking officers who supported the government were cultivated and
flattered by aristocratic civilians who had never before treated
military men as social equals. On the other hand, officers with
Liberal sympathies were often purged or sent to serve in the Colombian battalion stationed in Korea (1951-1953).

Nevertheless, by 1952, the armed forces had become deeply dis-
satisfied with the difficult and partisan role that the Conservative

governments had demanded from them. La Violencia held no prospect of ending soon. In fact, the Conservative Party itself was increasingly divided between pro-Gómez and more moderate pro-Ospina Perez factions. Many Conservatives withdrew their support from the government as Gómez began to intimidate his intra-party opposition.

In this praetorian context of civilian institutional failure, eventual military intervention was almost a certainty. Divided against itself, the civilian elite was unable to maintain minimal public order; however, because the armed forces were not yet highly professionalized nor psychologically prepared for sustained military rule, they did not execute a coup d'état until the Gómez government, in a sense, forced them to do so in June of 1953. Laureano Gómez had perceived the growing potential for military intervention and already had begun to plot against popular armed forces chief General Gustavo Rojas Pinilla who was suspected of being linked to the moderate faction of the Conservative Party. After a series of unsuccessful measures, ultimately Gómez tried to force acting-President Roberto Urdaneta Arbaláez to dismiss Rojas. Upon Urdaneta's refusal, Gómez reassumed the powers of the Presidency on June 13, 1953, but was deposed later the same day by a broadly supported bloodless coup that placed Rojas in power.[3] A century of military obedience to civilian authority had ended.

The military government began very successfully. General Rojas promised to institute a nonpartisan regime and offered full amnesty to guerrillas who would disarm. Consequently there was a large reduction in rural violence and Liberal leaders in exile began to return to the country. Quickly, however, Rojas' initial success and popularity dissipated during the next few months. It was not long before Rojas' preference for the Conservative Party became conspicuous. When the nonpartisan pretense was eliminated, the regime confronted much more opposition especially in the Liberal press. The government also faced considerable civilian criticism because of extravagant spending on the armed forces. Moreover, Rojas showed no inclination to give up the Presidency in the near future. Indeed, in order to stay in power, the General contemplated the creation of a Peronist-inspired mass political movement of the lower classes that clearly posed a threat to both traditional parties. Rojas stepped up his verbal attacks on the civilian political class and cultivated mass support through the activities of the Secretariado Nacional de Asistencia Social (SENDAS), a multi-purpose social welfare agency.

Rojas' attempts to build this personal base of support alienated many officers and virtually all of the civilian politicians in both parties (Fluharty, 1957). When the flow of revenue from high coffee prices ended, Rojas was unable to sustain the level of governmental expenditure that these programs and adventures required. The economic situation deteriorated rapidly and the government's ability to manage the nation's finances was questioned. These developments in addition to the military government's inability to completely stop rural violence, which in reality was rising again in 1956, led to general public disaffection with Rojas' increasingly authoritarian regime and helped to generate the inter-party elite compromise that created the National Front. When Rojas interfered with the legal electoral process in 1957, he was deposed by a military junta.

Obviously the Colombian military of the 1950's had not been adequately prepared as an institution to offer a genuine governmental alternative to the civilian elite. The armed forces lacked the requisite governmental expertise, institutional policy consensus, or corporate identity for such a role. The institution's expanded activities during La Violencia had not compensated for its earlier weakness and sense of inferiority, vis-à-vis the civilian elites. Thus, after having been forced to take power by circumstances, the "government of the armed forces" degenerated into a personalistic dictatorship that many officers found embarrassing. When the civilian politicians reconciled their differences, most of the military were relieved to return to traditional duties. The military junta, under provisional-President General Gabriel París, acted as a highly cooperative caretaker-government while assisting Liberal and Conservative leaders in the transition to the National Front. In 1958, when a few pro-Rojas officers attempted to disrupt the first National Front elections by capturing Presidential candidate Alberto Lleras Camargo and members of the military junta, the bulk of the armed forces refused to participate. Loyal troops quickly arrested the military conspirators and the elections were held on schedule.

THE MILITARY AND THE NATIONAL FRONT

Although the National Front arrangement eventually proved successful, its effectiveness was very much in doubt during the early 1960's. The outlook seemed particularly unfavorable when the administration of Conservative Guillermo León Valencia (1962-1966) performed poorly in the midst of falling exports, a weakening economy, and continuing rural violence. The partisan divisions responsible for La Violencia had decreased; but with socio-economic unrest intensifying, Colombia seemed to be drifting toward a new and more dangerous form of praetorian instability. This apparent deterioration in civilian governmental capability coincided with important institutional developments within the military that caused some officers to adopt a broader concept of their professional mission. Although this new current of military opinion, potentially so threatening to the civilian political elite, never became dominant within the officer corps even in these difficult times, it was significant enough to briefly disturb civil-military relations during the latter part of President Valencia's term.

The armed forces principal function in this period continued to be one of controlling rural violence. Some armed groups of the La Violencia epoch had never disbanded and had turned, instead, to non-political banditry. In addition, other small guerrilla groups had developed Marxist orientations during La Violencia and had established self-contained "independent republics" in inaccessible regions, e.g., Marquetalia in Tolima. As the military moved to eradicate these problems, the institution increased in size and became more professionalized. The key figure responsible for these institutional changes and for the attempts to develop

a new professional identity within the armed forces was General
Alberto Ruiz Novoa who served as army commander and later as Minister of War in President Valencia's Cabinet (1962-1965).

Like other members of Colombia's upper middle class, General
Ruiz had been attracted by a military career during the brief
surge of national patriotism that occurred at the time of the
Colombia-Peru conflict of the 1930's (Maingot, 1970: 174). Ruiz
later served with distinction as the commander of Colombian troops
in Korea and as Comptroller General in the Rojas government. He
was, therefore, unusually well known and respected when he at
last took command of the army. Ruiz quickly began to improve officer recruitment and training. A public relations firm was engaged
to raise the public image of the military career and the curriculum
of the Escuela Militar was revised and enlarged. Cadets now normal-
ly completed the final two years of secondary school at the academy
and, then, for the last three years of their training, specialized
in university-level engineering or economics (Maingot, 1970: 153).
Furthermore, Ruiz encouraged the military to engage in a broader
analysis of Colombia's social and economic problems; consequently,
the number of social science courses at both the academy and the
Escuela Superior de Guerra was greatly increased. General Ruiz
also employed the military's professional journals, Revista del
Ejército and Revista de las Fuerzas Armadas, as a means to raise
socio-economic awareness and professional standards within the
armed forces.

Most Colombian politicians supported these professionalization
measures because a strong armed forces was needed to combat disorder. The civilian elite also favored the institutional expansion
of the military. Between 1961 and 1965, the armed forces grew from
under 23,000 to over 37,000 men. Military expenditures rose from
about 17% to over 20% of the governmental budget (Statesman's
Yearbook, 1960-1965; Villegas, 1972: 187-189).[4]

The larger more professional military effectively brought the
rural disorder under control by means of a U.S. inspired counterinsurgency program. The anti-guerrilla strategy combined armed
repression with extensive civic action projects that were designed

to improve rural living conditions. Rural Colombia became more peaceful as the majority of the essentially non-political groups were dispersed or disbanded. In addition, between 1962 and 1965, the military, under General Ruiz's Plan Lazo, was able to subjugate the Marxist "independent republics" by employing fully one-third of its forces.

The military's successful counterinsurgency program stood in sharp contrast to the civilian government's economic and social failures. In this context and with Marxist guerrilla units active throughout Latin America, Ruiz began publicly to criticize the civilian political elite for its inability to deal with the underlying problems of economic underdevelopment and social inequality which made guerrilla movements possible. Ruiz (1965: 122, 125) noted that

> Colombia will not be great nor important while the great majority of its people continue to find themselves in a state of misery and ignorance....the country in its present circumstances finds itself up a blind alley. Its administration, its finances, its private economy, the traditional political parties, are in an obvious disorder....

The War Minister complained that the Valencia government in which he served lacked a sense of national purpose. He insisted strongly that the military should have a much larger and more independent role in the nation's socioeconomic development process. Ruiz (1965: 122) argued that in contrast to Colombian military tradition, the army's role was now "....not only to win battles but also to contribute to the betterment of the living conditions of the common people."

The civilian political elite became very worried about Ruiz's demands for fundamental socioeconomic changes and for a more independent military. Finally, in early January 1965, Ruiz overreached himself. With a major urban strike imminent, Ruiz began to meet privately with various civilian and military leaders. Rumors circulated to the effect that the General intended to take "emergency" powers to deal with the crisis. Although Ruiz later denied any plans to seize such powers, his suspicious behavior and earlier controversial statements were enough to convince

President Valencia to demand his resignation.[5] Neither Ruiz nor
any units under his command offered resistance to the President's
decision. After Ruiz was replaced by General Rebéiz Pizarro, social reformist or anti-civilian elite statements by military officers rarely appeared in the military journals or in any other context.

Thus, counterinsurgency theories and experiences which according to Stepan provided the basis for highly active, institutionalized military regimes elsewhere in Latin America during the 1960's
did have an effect on the Colombian military. However, the civil-
military tensions that arose proved much less serious in Colombia
and did not result in a military coup. Ruiz Novoa, whatever his
actual intentions might have been, was unable to lead the Colombian military into politics.

Many officers apparently felt that Ruiz was acting in his own
interest rather than in the interest of the armed forces. Ruiz's
personal ambitions alienated some members of the officer corps
while he caused others to dislike him for the rigid military program (Leal Buitrago, 1970: 193). More importantly, only a minority of the officer corps shared Ruiz's reformist views and fewer
officers desired, as he did, to expand the military's traditional
role at the expense of the civilian political elite. Although civilian politicians were facing serious problems including the exhaustion of the import substitution economic strategy, they were
still regarded by the majority of Colombians as the nation's legitimate rulers. In addition, most officers probably expected the
civilian elite to improve upon its recent governmental performance.
The drift toward a praetorian condition was, in fact, arrested
relatively quickly under the succeeding government of President
Carlos Lleras Restrepo (1966-1970) which increased governmental
capabilities and reoriented the economy toward export promotion.
The civilian governmental inadequacies would have to have been
more serious and more persistent to have made military intervention
a credible alternative. In comparison, O'Donnell (1976) shows that
the political situation that eventually resulted in the Argentine
military's professionalization drive and in the coup of 1966 was

much more volatile because of the much higher modernization pressures and also far more hopeless in light of greater civilian political factionalization. Thus military professionalization had both different causes and different effects in Colombia.

It should also be noted that the military's traditionally low prestige and lack of corporate identity had largely persisted despite Ruiz's professionalization measures and the counterinsurgency experience (Maingot, 1970: 181). Some officers no doubt were intrigued by Ruiz's notion of a modernizing military but the vast majority of the officer corps felt unsuited and unprepared for such a role. The military still lacked necessary governmental skills as it had so aptly demonstrated during the recent Rojas regime. In addition, no clear institutional conception of the solutions demanded by the nation's social or economic problems existed. Although military education had improved, there was no genuine Colombian counterpart to Brazil's Escola Superior de Guerra (ESG) or Peru's Centro de Altos Estudios Militares (CAEM) that could have created a strong military identity or a new sense of mission.

After his dismissal, Ruiz himself noted (Maingot, 1970: 168) the historically limited role of the armed forces that he had been unable to alter.

> During the present century the Colombian civilian ruling class has kept the military institution and its members in a state of complete submission. A constant indoctrination concerning the intellectual, social and political superiority of the civilians has been carried out which has produced an inferiority complex in the military.

Although the armed forces had clearly become more professionalized under Ruiz, they never developed a strong institutional ideology or sense of corporate unity. The military lacked the institutional strength to protect its highest ranking officers from civilian attack and humiliation. For example, in 1965, a few months after Ruiz's dismissal, the head of the Colombian air force, General Hermán Medina Mendoza, was tried and publicly disgraced in the mass media because of his alleged involvement in a minor smuggling incident (Icenhour, 1976: 151-153). Although absolved of guilt,

General Medina was retired from active duty without serious dis-
sension from within the armed forces. In short, the strength of
civilian political institutions continued to inhibit the development of an independent, unified military institution. The traditional pattern of civil-military relations remained intact.

During the later years of the National Front, the civilian
political elite greatly improved its ability to manage the economy
and the compromise program of defensive social reform. Although
the ANAPO movement posed an apparent danger to the National Front
for several years, the civilian elites retained sufficient legitimacy to govern and then watched ANAPO's support disintegrate between 1970 and 1974. As Colombia moved away from the praetorian
potential of the early 1960's, civil-military relations became
very smooth. The armed forces again expanded to meet new Marxist
guerrilla threats; however, this continued institutional expansion
and professionalization did not lead to the development of an au-
tonomous military institution. The military remained one of the
most important instruments of the civilian political elite.

During the latter part of the National Front era, the military
principally confronted two new Marxist guerrilla organizations, the
Ejército de Liberación Nacional (ELN) and the Fuerzas Armadas
Revolucionarias Colombianas (FARC), in rural Colombia. The student-
led ELN, composed of an estimated three hundred actives, was Castro-
ite in orientation and usually conducted operations in rural Santander, Antioquia, and Bolívar. The ELN attained some international
notoriety when, in 1965, well-known radical priest Camilo Torres
joined its ranks although he was to be killed shortly thereafter.
The less homogenous FARC, on the other hand, although supported
by the regular Communist Party, was composed largely of less ideologically sophisticated guerrilla groups surviving from the La
Violencia era. Operating primarily in Tolima and south-central
Colombia, the FARC was estimated to be larger than the ELN.

The armed forces relied heavily on armed repression to deal
with these new guerrillas although a few civic action programs were
maintained. By the end of the National Front period, the army had
severely reduced the guerrillas' ability to carry out major oper-

ations against the government. Neither the ELN nor FARC ever posed a serious danger to the National Front's survival because of the guerrillas' inability to generate popular peasant support in rural Colombia. Moreover, the military's successful counter-guerrilla activity reduced the ability of the guerrillas to discredit the civilian government with frequent outbreaks of rural disorder. The armed forces also assisted the civilian government by suppressing various striking groups that occasionally threatened violence in urban areas. In addition, military courts were responsible for the prosecution of public order violators under the state-of-siege laws usually in effect.

As noted above, the civilian political elite continued to enlarge and professionalize the armed forces during the later years of the National Front. The armed forces increased to 64,000 men (2,600 officers) in the late 1960's and have remained approximately at this level in succeeding years. The total figure given encompasses the 8,000-man navy and 6,000-man air force but does not reflect an additional 35,000-man national police force which is actually under military control. Budgetary expenditures on the military fluctuated considerably between 1966 and 1974 registering a low of 1.0% and a high of 2.5% of GNP (World Military, 1976: 25). Various sources show some discrepancies with respect to the size of the armed forces budget in specific years but most seem to agree that overall military expenditures increased during this period at least enough to accommodate the greater number of men under arms. Although the Colombian military remained rather small relative to population and under-financed compared to the Argentine, Chilean, and Peruvian militaries, the institution had become a much more substantial physical force than it had been in the past (Maullin, 1973: 85-87, 91, 95; Heare, 1971: 8). Moreover, the Colombian military had become particularly well equipped with counter-guerrilla weaponry that was most appropriate to its recent mission, e.g., small arms, helicopters. Only after the guerrilla threat subsided in the early 1970's were military expenditures directed toward the purchase of more sophisticated weapons such as fifteen French Mirage M-5 jets and a German-constructed submarine.

The military educational system also grew to accommodate the
new recruit influx. All new conscripts (16,000 to 20,000 per year)
received a twenty-six week military training course, a basic pri-
mary education, and some rudimentary occupational training, e.g.,
construction trades (Studer, 1975: 245). After 1968,
noncommissioned officers' education was also institutionalized
with the creation of a three-year NCP school in Popayán. Officers
continued to benefit from the professional educational system improved by General Ruiz Novoa in the 1960's although the attempt in
1971 to turn the Escuela Militar into a regular four-year university accepting only high school graduates failed because of insuf-
ficient applications (Studer, 1975: 300). In 1976, there were over
350 Colombian military officers training in U.S. Army military in-
stallations and all officers were required to complete the U.S.
inspired counterinsurgency course at the Escuela de Lanceros before
being promoted to first lieutenant (Blutstein, 1977: 440). Finally,
one should note that the armed forces continued to enjoy reasonably
good salaries and fringe benefits under the National Front. Salaries regularly kept pace with inflation and extra benefits included
free hospitalization, substantial pensions, and subsidized housing.
The average Colombian officer was generally able to maintain a moderate middle class standard of living equivalent to that of a middle
level public official.

The Colombian military had indeed become larger and more pro-
fessionally competent under the National Front; however, it never
developed a strong sense of corporate identity or institutional
unity. Although morale within the officer corps was better than
it had been in the past, the institution still suffered from the
fact that the military career did not carry high social prestige.
Icenhour (1976: 215) shows that the officer corps is recruited
largely from the middle and lower middle classes. Moreover, he
demonstrates that few new officers are inducted from military
families. Where the military has a high sense of corporate identity as it does in Argentina, Brazil, and Peru, the officer corps
clearly has this self-perpetuating aspect. However, in Colombia,
former officers consider the military career less attractive for

their sons than many alternative civilian occupations. Icenhour's
(1976) survey of four hundred <u>Escuela Militar</u> students in 1972
shows that only 5% had military officers for fathers.

Not only did the military obediently defend the National Front
during its last two administrations but also it refrained from
Ruiz-like statements or interference in politics. Except for one
minor incident in 1960 when President Lleras Restrepo ousted army
commander General Pinzón Caicedo because of an article in a military journal which expressed dissatisfaction with civilian scrutiny
of the military budget, the military avoided any activity that would
lead to civil-military tension. Although a number of social reformists remained in the military, the concern for Colombia's socio-
economic inequalities that General Ruiz Novoa had shown was replaced in the military periodicals by numerous articles that em-
phasized hard-line anti-communism. Military authors exhibited an
affinity for the more right-wing military regimes of Latin America
and explicitly rejected the Peruvian model of military-directed
social reform (See Durán, 1971: 13-14). Minister of Defense General Ayerbe Chaux (1967-1970), for example, saw the communist threat
to Colombia in very broad terms. He once wrote (Ayerbe Chaux,
1965: 238) that

> it (communism) is a palpitating reality which has for
> some years been manifesting itself by means of intense,
> copious and well-directed propaganda, by the methodical
> agitation of different social sectors, by various front
> organizations, by the infiltration into the university,
> the high schools and into different state and private
> organizations, and finally by the guerrilla movements....

In the 1970's, on the other hand, some military officers
sought to reduce the appeal of the guerrillas by questioning the
movements' ideological credentials.[6] In 1973, General Luis Carlos
Camacho Leyva (<u>El Tiempo</u>, October 20, 1973) dismissed both the ELN
and FARC by stating that "... rebellion does not exist in Colombia,
only banditry."

In light of the military's increasingly hard-line position,
many began to regard the armed forces as the National Front's potential bulwark against the ANAPO populism during the years when
the movement appeared to be a serious problem (See Deas, 1973: 88;

Solaún and Cepeda, 1973: 94-96). A few retired and noncommissioned officers were pro-ANAPO because the movement promised increased military benefits but most of the officer corps was never attracted to ANAPO. Some superior officers may have worried that Rojas would settle old scores by dismissing those individuals who had supported his own ouster in 1957. Most officers preferred the competent National Front leadership perhaps because the ANAPO movement was too reminiscent of other Latin American populisms which previously had endangered possibilities for economic development and political order. When the 1970 election results were disputed, the armed forces demonstrated their loyalty by suppressing ANAPO rioters and by holding Rojas under house arrest.

THE MILITARY UNDER LÓPEZ AND TURBAY

The basic patterns of military behavior and civil-military relations that characterized the late National Front have been maintained under the governments of Liberal Presidents Alfonso López Michelsen[7] and Julio César Turbay Ayala since the formal conclusion of the National Front era in 1974. The civilian political elite's capability and legitimacy have persisted, hence, the armed forces have continued to defend the legal civilian government from various rural and urban disorders.

Under López Michelsen, the armed forces once again became deeply engaged in counter-guerrilla warfare. The guerrilla organizations seemed to be on the verge of disintegration in the last year of the National Front after the army had made a concerted effort to destroy them. The ELN, for example, was particularly impaired by the army's 1973 Operación Anori which resulted in the death of two of the Vásquez Castaño brothers who were its leaders. However, between 1975 and 1978, the Colombian guerrillas staged a resurgence which forced the army to increase counterinsurgency actions. Military civic action projects, including the construction of clinics, schools, and roads, were undertaken in some of the guerrilla zones, e.g., Meta, Bolívar, Antioquia, but the army continued to rely mainly on armed repression to deal with guerrillas.

The ELN executed several kidnappings of wealthy or prominent people and ambushed army patrols. This guerrilla group was especially active in remote southern Bolívar where it had been able to overrun a few small villages temporarily. However, the military actually was more persistently involved with the FARC during the López years. In Puerto Rico in Caquetá in 1975, about 200 FARC guerrillas robbed the local bank, stole provisions, and lectured the populace before helicopter-borne soldiers arrived to eject them (Latin America: Political Report, April 18, 1975). In 1976, FARC seizure of Sabana Grande in Santander merited national headlines. This movement also was active in Antioquia, Tolima, Magdalena, Boyacá, and Meta and staged its own spectacular killings. Although the armed forces were able to keep both of these guerrilla organizations from posing any real threat to the López Michelsen government, the ELN and FARC were active enough to cause embarrassment. The guerrillas might have become more of a nuisance to the government but they were unable to unite in support of a single political program. A third guerrilla organization, the Ejército Popular de Liberación, which, since 1974, has become active enough to be taken seriously also is unable to unite with either of the two more important guerrilla movements because of allegedly Maoist orientations. In 1975, the army located and eliminated the EPL's founder, Pedro León Arboleda, in Cali.

In addition, public order was upset during the López Michelsen administration by workers striking violently against the government's strict austerity program and by students who demonstrated in their support. The armed forces were employed by the government to repress both types of disruption. In early 1975, Minister of Defense General Varón Valencia publicly admonished potential strikers that the army stood ready to repress any threats to the nation's democratic institutions. In November 1975, troops were deployed against striking sugar workers in the Cauca Valley and the armed forces often were used in similar ways during succeeding years, e.g., ECOPETROL petroleum workers strike. The army also invaded a number of universities to quell student disorders throughout this period at the behest of the government.

Finally, although the military's most important role has been
to maintain public order during the difficult months of López
Michelsen's austerity plan, the regular armed forces have been used
by the government in a variety of other ways. For example, the
military continues to undertake colonization and civil defense projects begun during the National Front period and has been employed
to control drug, emerald, and coffee smuggling.

The Colombian military served the López Michelsen government
well. Moreover, the pattern of secure civilian control over the
armed forces has persisted since the end of the National Front era.
The events surrounding the dismissal of army commander General
Álvaro Valencia Tovar in June 1975, the single important civil-
military incident of the López Michelsen administration, further
confirms the traditional pattern of military subordination to the
civilian political elite.

General Álvaro Valencia Tovar was one of the most highly respected officers in the Colombian armed forces. After proving his
professional abilities as a young captain in Korea, Valencia Tovar
distinguished himself as a major military voice for social reform
during General Ruiz Novoa's tenure as Minister of War. In 1962,
Valencia Tovar authored a controversial internal report for Ruiz
which argued that the military should develop greater institutional
independence from the traditional parties in order to be more
effective in the rural guerrilla war (Maingot, 1970: 167). Although Conservative congressmen obtained the report and clamored
for Valencia Tovar's dismissal, he remained in his post. In fact,
Valencia Tovar continued to press for a social reformist response
to the guerrilla problem even after Ruiz's dismissal revealed
reformism to be a minority position within the military. His novel,
Uisheda (Valencia Tovar, 1969), written during the 1960's, demonstrates a sophisticated and sympathetic understanding of the socio-
economic causes behind guerrilla warfare. Although a reformist,
Valencia Tovar continued to advance rapidly in his military career
on the basis of his intelligence and professionalism and perhaps
also because he had never advocated the greatly expanded military
role associated with Ruiz. In the early 1970's he was commandant

of the Escuela Militar.

After López Michelsen was elected President, General Valencia
Tovar became the head of the army making him the third highest ranking officer in the armed forces. Many commentators felt that reformist Valencia Tovar would soon be chosen as the appropriate
Minister of Defense for the reformist López even though the General's political views continued to represent a minority position
within the armed forces hierarchy. One of Valencia Tovar's first
actions as commander of the army was to organize a joint civilian-
military seminar in Antioquia in order to discuss the nation's
social and educational problems and cultivate support for the government. However, less than a year later, López demanded Valencia
Tovar's resignation. Although we can dismiss reports of an impend-
ing military coup d'état, the actual reasons for the Valencia Tovar
resignation are still in doubt.

Events seem to have been set in motion in April 1975 when
illness prevented General Efraín Vallejo Ardila from accepting his
new position as Inspector General of the armed forces. General
Puyana García, head of the Brigade of Military Institutes (BIM)
in Bogotá, received orders to take the post in place of Valleja
Ardila. Although this theoretically represented an advancement
for Puyana García, the so-called promotion actually withdrew him
from a prestigious field command and placed him in a purely administrative position. Not surprisingly, Puyana García, who had held
his command for only a few months, was irate. He asked his friend
and superior Valencia Tovar, who apparently had not been consulted
with respect to the command shift, to intercede for him with the
President and Minister of Defense. These efforts were unsuccessful
and Puyana García apparently began to consider voluntary retirement.

Puyana García's subordinates in the BIM were dismayed by their
highly respected commander's undeserved fate. Some officers, particularly the head of the infantry school, Lieutenant Colonel
Valentín Jiménez Caravajal, became too vocal in their criticism
of the Minister of Defense, General Varón Valencia, for his role
in the affair. In swift retaliation for this supposed insubordin-
ation, the Minister of Defense ordered the immediate retirement

of both Puyana García and Jiménez Caravajal. Evidently Varón
Valencia also again violated customary military courtesy by acting
before consulting the officers' superior, Valencia Tovar, who was
at that time, meeting with his Venezuelan counterpart in the border
town of Arauca (Latin America: Political Report, May 30, 1975).
Furthermore, the Minister of Defense transferred a number of officers out of the BIM and temporarily confined the military police
and presidential guard to their barracks.

The Defense Minister's actions prompted El Occidente, a Conservative Cali newspaper, to speculate on the possible coup intentions of the dismissed officers. In response to this and other
media-inspired rumors, both Valencia Tovar and Minister of Defense
Varón Valencia issued statements in which they vehemently denied
the various coup stories; however, their statements were very different in tone. Although the Minister of Defense still charged
the two former officers with "grave indiscipline," army commander
Valencia Tovar defended Puyana García and Jiménez Caravajal ar-
guing that they had at no time engaged in acts disloyal to the institutions. President Lopez found this discrepancy between the two
public statements by these high ranking officers unacceptable;
therefore, much to everyone's surprise, he dismissed General
Valencia Tovar on May 27 and replaced him with army second-in-
command, General Luis Carlos Camacho Leyva.

Some sources suggest that this series of events was essentially
accidental and that the confrontation between Valencia Tovar and
the Minister of Defense was an involuntary one that López simply
chose to end by ousting the junior of the two officers (See Visión,
June 15, 1975). Other sources, however, maintain that the chain
of events was purposely designed to result in the dismissal of
the reformist officers involved. It has been implied by some that
López may have become uncertain about the willingness of Valencia
Tovar and other reformists such as Puyana García to use the force
necessary to suppress violent worker and student opposition that
was generated by the economic austerity measures (See Latin America:
Political Report, June 13, 1975). Thus López and hard-line officers,
e.g., Varón Valencia, may have deliberately displaced Puyana García

without consulting Valencia Tovar precisely in order to provoke
protests from both officers that could be used as excuses for their
dismissals. A somewhat different interpretation has been offered
in the Colombian Marxist journal, Alternativa, which also links
these incidents to López's economic emergency measures (Alternativa,
June 2-8, 1975). The journal argues that the climate of unrest
which resulted from this economic policy instigated many coup rumors in civilian political circles. Although most civilian politicians doubted such rumors, López was persuaded to take the pre-
cautionary measure of removing the reformist Puyana García from
the strategic BIM command reasoning that if a military threat ever
did materialize, it would come from the army's reformist faction.
This action thus implicitly impugned the loyalty of Puyana García
and his unconsulted superior Valencia Tovar and, therefore, was
almost certain to result in their retirements either by voluntary
choice or by dismissal for an insubordinate statement.

Whether the Valencia Tovar dismissal was unplanned or engi-
neered, the aspect of the incident that is most interesting from
a comparative perspective is that the dismissal of this prestigious
officer passed so quietly. A few middle-ranking and junior officers
also supposedly associated with the reformist minority within the
military were retired shortly thereafter but no opposition of any
type was offered to this civilian interference in the armed forces
hierarchy.[8] Civilian action had essentially reinforced the conservative political leanings of the military majority. Valencia
Tovar, upon being returned to civilian status, accepted the out-
come quietly, and, in August 1975, began a regular editorial col-
umn in the principal Liberal newspaper, El Tiempo, from which he
continues to express his reformist views. In 1978 the former
General was an unsuccessful independent candidate for President.

The Colombian armed forces have continued to lack the type
of corporate autonomy necessary to insulate themselves from civilian interference. Traditional low military prestige has contributed
to this lack of autonomy. Moreover, other events that occurred
during the López regime demonstrate that the armed forces' image
has not been improving. For example, there were repeated public

charges of corruption among high ranking officers. In 1976, the
government began an investigation of National Police Commander,
General Henry García Bohórquez, for alleged mismanagement of police
funds. At the same time, government prosecutors were investigating
other officers, including former air force commander General José
Ramón Calderón Molano, for supposedly accepting a $200,000 bribe
from Lockheed Aircraft. Other officers were suspected of acquiring
similar bribes from West German and French arms manufacturers and
in 1978 former Internal Security (DAS) Chief General Jorge Ordóñez
Valderrama was sentenced to seven years in prison for embezzlement.
The army's reputation was further damaged during the López period
by the spectacular trial of the alleged ELN assassins of Inspector
General, General Ramón Rincón Quiñones, in which the defense
claimed that superior officers had ordered the General killed in
order to halt his investigation of corruption at INDUMIL, the military's industrial company. In an El Tiempo editorial, now retired
General Valencia Tovar lamented the fact that corruption had brought
the armed forces' image to a new low (El Tiempo, February 19, 1976).[9]

Colombian civil-military relations have undergone no major
changes during the initial eighteen months of the Turbay administration. The army continued to defend the civilian elite by opposing
the rural guerrilla movements and by successfully containing the
threat of M-19, a new urban guerrilla organization that shocked the
country in early 1979 by raiding a major military arsenal in Bogotá.[10] Armed with a new, tougher internal security statute, the
military relentlessly pursued suspected members of the M-19 under-
ground as well as other supposed subversives, e.g., (MAO) Movimiento
de Autodefensa Obrera. As a result, most of the arms stolen from
the Bogotá arsenal were quickly recovered and hundreds of arrests
took place.

The establishment press praised the soldiers for their swift
and effective action against these dangerous new guerrilla elements.
However, the military's heavy-handed use of the new security legis-
lation also resulted in the indiscriminate detention of many prominent Leftist journalists, artists, and scholars such as sociologist
Orlando Fals Borda and 75 year-old Luis Vidales whose connection

to M-19 was considered doubtful. In addition, many prisoners ac-
cused the units of the BIM (Brigade of Military Institutes) of
using torture during interrogation. These claims stimulated the
Colombian Left and some opposition politicians in both the Liberal
and Conservative parties to increase their criticism of President
Turbay and his new Defense Minister General Luis Carlos Camacho
Leyva for human rights violations (Latin America: Political Report,
February 16, 1979).

Some angry commentators went as far as to suggest that the
armed forces were using this new situation to gain control of
Colombian politics at the expense of the traditional civilian
authorities (New York Times, November 14, 1979). Although President Turbay felt compelled to deny these allegations publicly, they
seem to have little real foundation. Though obviously troubling,
the recent urban guerrilla problem simply was not serious enough
or persistent enough to induce an Uruguayan-like pattern of grad-
ual military takeover. M-19 generated minimal popular support and
never posed the type of continuing embarrassment to civilian political elites that the Tupamaros represented in Uruguay.[11] The M-19
movement continued to gain world-wide media attention, however, with
its capture of the American ambassador and other diplomatic hos-
tages in February of 1980 by means of an armed assualt on a recep-
tion at the Dominican embassy in Bogotá.

CONCLUSIONS AND THE FUTURE

Although military government is the norm in Latin America,
Colombia continues to maintain a tradition of civilian control
over the armed forces. This paper has attempted to relate the
Colombian case to current theory in order to explain the Colombian
military's deviance from the contemporary norm of intervention.
The findings can be summarized briefly as follows. The Colombian
military remains obedient to civilian authority primarily because
the civilian political elite continues to demonstrate its unity,
its governmental capabilities, and its popular legitimacy. In
this respect, the analysis has shown that the National Front

experiment in bipartisan coalition government was a major success.
The praetorian atmosphere of political decay and of civilian institutional collapse that Huntington and others have associated with
modernization pressures in most Latin American nations is thus not
present in Colombia despite considerable social mobilization and
serious obstacles to economic growth and distribution. Civilian
failures have not proved serious enough or long enough in duration
to encourage the more professionalized Colombian armed forces of
today to reject their traditional role, much less to contemplate
an active, institutionalized regime on the Brazilian or Argentine
pattern discussed by O'Donnell.[12] Some officers such as Ruiz Novoa
and Valencia Tovar have been influenced by aspects of what Stepan
has termed the "new professionalism," but, even in the worst days
of the National Front, these officers held relatively modest con-
ceptions of rightful military influence and represented a distinct
minority within a military that still lacks a strong sense of corporate unity or identity.[13]

Nevertheless, Colombia's calm civil-military relations are
not certain to continue. Indeed, many factors suggest that the
civilian political elite will be severely tested in the next decade. Social mobilization is increasing; literacy is rising and
peasants continue to migrate to Colombia's urban centers at alarm-
ing rates. Time may also erode some of the factors discussed above
that have rendered mass demands manageable until now. Memories of
La Violencia, for example, must one day begin to fade. In addition,
the children of earlier urban migrants will come of age in the
cities and may be more available for political organization than
were their peasant parents. In short, the potential for greatly
increased societal demands for redistribution clearly exists.
The Colombian economy, on the other hand, indicates no such potential for growth and expansion. Export dependency, low agricultural
productivity, and a semi-developed industrial sector indicate a
precarious economic future that is further darkened by Colombia's
population growth. It is possible that careful governmental management and favorable export prices will result in better economic
performance than expected, but, although this may be the case,

rising social mobilization and poor income distribution patterns
suggest that the imbalance between mass demands and their fulfill-
ment will increase nonetheless.

As Colombia approaches the higher modernization level described
by O'Donnell, the civilian political elites may find orthodox economic policies more difficult to impose on the populace. Party
identification ties also may begin to weaken; indeed the abstention
votes of 1978 suggest that the process may already be underway.
In such a context, Colombian Presidents may find it necessary to
confront the impossible choices that many other Latin American
civilian leaders have faced already. Some future Colombian leaders
will choose economic austerity and accept higher levels of civil
violence and opposition while others may turn to inflationary
populism. If the civilian elite can maintain competency and legitimacy in the troubled times ahead, the traditional pattern of
Colombian civil-military relations will continue. The Colombian
army will remain like the Mexican military as a major support of
the civilian elite. However, if Colombia lapses into the praetorian condition, military intervention will become a distinct possi-
bility. Persistent economic deterioration and rising urban guerrilla violence could gradually undermine traditional civil-military
relations as in the case of Uruguay.

If the Colombian military does take control of the government
again, the armed forces probably will act in a conservative fashion
in order to reduce popular pressures. As in the Brazilian experience, the high level of social mobilization should convince the
armed forces hierarchy that the institution is most immediately
endangered by the forces of the Left. The dismissal of social
reformists such as Ruiz Novoa and Valencia Tovar has already placed
the military firmly in the hands of conservative officers. The
likelihood that the Colombian military, once in power, would attempt
to institute major changes in Colombian society following the
Brazilian or Argentine model of Bureaucratic-authoritarian rule,
e.g., social conflict suppression, deactivation of dissident
political groups, technocratic development policy, would depend
on the duration and severity of the praetorian conditions that

induced intervention. A longer, more serious period of civilian institutional failure would be necessary for the process of military institutional unification and change that O'Donnell has documented in the Argentine case to take place particularly in light of the traditionally weak sense of corporate identity in the Colombian military.[14]

Colombian civil-military relations are currently atypical of Latin America. Although military governments rule most countries in the region, Colombia remains one of the very few nations in which civilian rule persists. Nonetheless, as modernization progresses and the Colombian civilian elite faces increasing socio-economic pressures, the durability of the traditional civil-military relationship described here will become much less certain. The Chilean and Uruguayan experiences demonstrate how quickly traditional military roles can change in contemporary Latin America.

NOTES

1. Praetorianism or political decay can also result because of civilian political conflicts that have little to do with problems of social mobilization. Latin America in the 19th century experienced considerable political decay while still a very traditional society. The social mobilization pressures that Huntington emphasizes, however, seem to have a great deal to do with praetorian conditions in contemporary Latin America.

2. The role of the army in this period is dealt with at greater length in Ruhl (1980). In general, the brief historical section of this paper draws upon the earlier analysis.

3. Gómez had formally stepped aside due to illness allowing Undaneta to carry out the official functions of the Presidency although Gómez continued to hold the real power. On this period, see Simpson (1968).

4. The figures cited in Maullin (1973: 83) are somewhat different. Official Colombian military expenditure statistics vary considerably from one source to another and are not

considered highly reliable (See Appendix B).

5. Studer (1975: 178-179) notes that the Ruiz dismissal
was suggested to President Valencia by General Rebéiz Pizarro,
Ruiz's immediate subordinate, after consultations with other
high ranking officers of the Colombian army, navy, and air force.
Studer also cites the personal frictions between Ruiz and Rebéiz
Pizarro although he does not feel that these animosities were
responsible for the incident.

6. The official periodicals best reflect the attitudes of
the military's highest ranking officers. Support for Peruvian-
style reformism as practiced by General Velasco in the late
1960's may, of course, exist elsewhere in the officer corps.
It should also be noted that the "conservative" military regimes
differ considerably from one another, e.g., "decompression" in
Brazil contrasts with continued repression in Chile in 1980.

7. López Michelsen is the son of former President López
Pumarejo who is discussed above. The defeated Conservative
candidate Álvaro Gómez is the son of former Colombian President
Laureano Gómez.

8. In a much less significant incident, López dismissed
reputedly reformist General José Joaquín Matallana from the army
in late 1977.

9. On the Rincón Quiñones case, see also Alternativa (September 13-20, 1976) and Latin America: Political Report (March 26,
1976). Incidentally, the ELN claimed to have executed Rincón but
also alleged that the defendants convicted by military court were
innocent.

10. M-19 designates the Movimiento de Abril 19 which claims
to have originated in the radical wing of ANAPO in response to
the "stolen" election of April 19, 1970 in which ANAPO's candidate
General Rojas was allegedly deprived of his victory. The movement
first gained national attention in 1974 by stealing the sword of
liberator Simón Bolívar. Since 1974, M-19 has engaged in kidnap-
ping, thefts, and other common urban guerrilla activities. Marxist
elements seem to figure in the movement but, given the lack of

information on the subject, little more can be stated definitely (See New York Times, March 10, 1980).

11. See Echeverry (1978) who also claims that Colombian politics is becoming increasingly militarized.

12. How professionalized has the Colombian military now become in comparison with other Latin American armed forces? This is a difficult factor to measure exactly but one authority has rated the region's militaries (with the exception of Cuba) as follows: (a) high professionalization--Argentina, Brazil, Peru, (b) moderate professionalization--Chile, Colombia, Mexico, Uruguay, Venezuela, (c) low professionalization--all other Latin American nations (Fitch, 1979: 375).

13. A good example of current military thinking is Landazábal Reyes (1975). This General was chosen to replace Puyana García at the BIM after the 1975 dismissals and was made chief of the joint general staffs in 1979.

14. This reasoning is also related to O'Donnell's (1978) recent work on the dynamics of bureaucratic-authoritarian regimes. For an excellent discussion and critique of O'Donnell's theory, see Collier (1978, 1979).

APPENDIX A

INDICATORS OF SOCIAL MOBILIZATION IN LATIN AMERICA, 1975-1976

	% URBAN	RANK	% LITERATE	RANK
ARGENTINA	83.2	1	92.6	2
BOLIVIA	31.6	18	59.5	15+
BRAZIL	62.7	7	81.2	7
CHILE	81.6	2	89.6	4
COLOMBIA	68.2	5	77.6	10
COSTA RICA	43.6	13	88.4	5
CUBA	62.0	8	97.0	1
DOMINICAN REPUBLIC	47.9	12	76.7	12
ECUADOR	42.6	14	75.0	14
EL SALVADOR	40.2	15	59.5	15+
GUATEMALA	31.2	19	47.3	19
HONDURAS	33.3	17	58.0	17
MEXICO	61.7	9	76.3	13
NICARAGUA	52.8	10	52.6	18
PANAMA	51.1	11	84.0	6
PARAGUAY	36.0	16	80.5	8
PERU	64.7	6	78.9	9
URUGUAY	80.8	3	89.8	3
VENEZUELA	74.6	4	77.1	11

Source: Inter-American Development Bank, Economic and Social
Progress in Latin America: 1976 Report as cited in
Wiarda and Kline (1979: 5).

APPENDIX B

COLOMBIAN MILITARY EXPENDITURES, 1950-1970

YEARS	SIZE OF FORCES 1.	EXPENDITURES IN U.S. DOLLARS* 2.	EXPENDITURES AS % GDP 3.
1950	14,660	27	1.1
1951	14,660	32	1.2
1952	15,660	43	1.6
1953	15,660	62	2.1
1954	15,660	65	2.0
1955	16,589	61	1.9
1956	16,589	62	1.8
1957	20,800	50	1.4
1958	20,800	48	1.4
1959	20,800	47	1.3
1960	20,800	57	1.4
1961	20,800	54	1.3
1962	22,800	56	1.3
1963	22,800	61	1.4
1964	22,800	62	1.3
1965	37,000	62	1.3
1966	53,500	65	1.3
1967	52,000	65	1.2
1968	64,000	86	1.5
1969	64,000	78	1.3
1970	64,000	96	1.5

* In millions of 1967 dollars

Sources: (1) The Statesman's Yearbook, 1953-1970, except for 1965-1967 found in Maullin (1973: 82), (2, 3) found in Heare (1971: 14).

49

REFERENCES

Ayerbe Chaux, G.
  1965   La amenaza communista. Revista del Ejército 5:237-240.

Bailey, J.J.
  1977   Pluralist and Corporatist Dimensions of Interest Representa-
         tion in Colombia. In J.M. Malloy, ed. Authoritarianism
         and Corporatism in Latin America. Pittsburgh, PA:
         University of Pittsburgh Press.

Berry, R.A. et al
  1980   Politics of Compromise; Coalition Government in Colombia.
         New Brunswick, NJ: Transaction Books.

Blutstein, H.I.
  1977   Area Handbook for Colombia. Washington, D.C.: United
         States Government Printing Office.

Bushnel, D.
  1971   Voter Participation in the Colombian Election of 1856.
         Hispanic American Historical Review 51:237-249.

Campos, J.T. and J.F. McCamant
  1972   Cleavage Shift in Colombia: Analysis of the 1970 Elections.
         Sage Comparative Politics Series 3.

Collier, D.
 · 1978   Industrial Modernization and Political Change: A Latin
         American Perspective. World Politics 30:593-614.

  1979   The New Authoritarianism in Latin America. Princeton, NJ:
         Princeton University Press.

Cornelius, W.A.
  1974   Urbanization and Political Demand Making: Political
         Participation Among the Urban Poor in Latin American
         Cities. American Political Science Review 68:1125-1146.

Deas, M.
  1973   Colombian Aprils. Current History 64:77-80, 88.

Dix, R.H.
  1967   Colombia: The Political Dimensions of Change.
         New Haven, CT: Yale University Press.

  1978   The Varieties of Populism: The Case of Colombia. Western
         Political Quarterly 31:334-351.

Durán, J.
  1971   Las Fuerzas armadas respetan las instituciones democráticas.
         Revista del Ejército 12:13-14.

Echeverry, A.
  1978   El poder y los militares: Un análisis de los ejércitos
         del continente y Colombia. Bogotá: Editorial Suramérica.

Einaudi, L.R.
1973   Revolution from Within?: Military Rule in Peru Since
        1968. Studies in Comparative International Development
        8:71-87.

Fals Borda, O.
1965   Violence and the Breakup of Tradition in Colombia. In
        C. Veliz, ed. Obstacles to Change in Latin America.
        Pp. 188-205. London: Oxford University Press.

Fitch, J.S.
1979   The Political Impact of U.S. Military Aid to Latin
        America. Armed Forces and Society 5:360-386.

Fluharty, V.
1957   The Dance of the Millions: Military Rule and Social
        Revolution in Colombia, 1930-1956. Pittsburgh, PA:
        University of Pittsburgh Press.

Garcés, J.
1972   Desarrollo político y desarrollo económico: los casos de
        Chile y Colombia. Madrid: Editorial Tecnos.

Gómez Buendía, H.
1978   Alfonso López Michelsen: un examen crítico de su
        pensamiento y de su obra de gobierno. Bogotá: Tercer
        Mundo.

Handelman, H.
1975   The Political Mobilization of Urban Squatter Settlements:
        Santiago's Experience and its Implications for Urban
        Research. Latin American Research Review 10:35-65.

Heare, G.E.
1971   Trends in Latin American Military Expenditures, 1940-1970.
        Washington,D.C.: United States Department of State.

Helguera, J.L.
1961   The Changing Role of the Military in Colombia. Journal
        of Inter-American Studies 3:351-358.

Hoskin, G.
1979   Post-National Front Trends in the Colombian Party System:
        More of the Same? Latin American Studies Association
        Conference Paper. Pittsburgh, PA.

Huntington, S.P.
1968   Political Order in Changing Societies. New Haven,CT:
        Yale University Press.

1957   The Soldier and the State. Cambridge, MA: Harvard
        University Press.

Icenhour, J.O.
1976   The Military in Colombian Politics. Ph.D. dissertation,
        George Washington University.

Landazábal Reyes, F.
1975   Factores de violencia. Bogotá: Tercer Mundo.

51

Leal Buitrago, F.
  1973 Análisis histórico del desarrollo político nacional,
        1930-1970. Bogotá: Tercer Mundo.

  1970 Política e intervención militar en Colombia. In
        R.P. Sandoval, ed. Dependencia externa y desarrollo
        político en Colombia. Pp. 155-207. Bogotá: Imprenta
        Nacional.

Lowenthal, A.E.
  1976 Armies and Politics in Latin America. New York: Holmes
        and Meier.

Maingot, A.P.
  1970 Colombia. In L.N. McAllster, ed. The Military in Latin
        American Socio-Political Evolution: Four Case Studies.
        Pp. 127-195. Washington, D.C.: American Institute for
        Research.

  1969 Social Structure, Social Status and Civil-Military
        Conflict in Urban Colombia, 1810-1850. In S. Therustrom
        and R. Sennett, eds. Nineteenth Century Cities: Essays
        in a New Urban History. Pp. 295-355. New Haven, CT:
        Yale University Press.

Mangin, W.
  1967 Latin American Squatter Settlements: A Problem and a
        Solution. Latin American Research Review 2: 65-98.

Martz, J.D.
  1962 Colombia: A Contemporary Survey. Chapel Hill, NC:
        University of North Carolina Press.

Maullin, R.
  1973 Soldiers, Guerrillas and Politics in Colombia.
        Lexington, MA: Lexington Books.

McDonald, R.H.
  1975 The Rise of Military Politics in Uruguay. Inter-American
        Economic Affairs 28:25-43.

O'Donnell, G.A.
  1973 Modernization and Bureaucratic-Authoritarianism: Studies
        in South American Politics. Berkeley, CA: University
        of California Press.

  1976 Modernization and Military Coups: Theory, Comparisons
        and the Argentine Case. In A. Lowenthal, ed. Armies and
        Politics in Latin America. Pp. 197-243. New York:
        Holmes and Meier.

  1978 Reflections on the Patterns of Change in the Bureaucratic-
        Authoritarian State. Latin American Research Review
        13:3-36.

Payne, J.
  1968 Patterns of Conflict in Colombia. New Haven, CT: Yale
        University Press.

Peattie, J.A.
1972 The View from the Barrio. Ann Arbor, MI: University of Michigan Press.

Peeler, J.A.
1976 Colombian Parties and Political Development: A Reassessment. Journal of Inter-American Studies 18:203-224.

Rueda Vargas, T.
1944 El ejército nacional. Bogota: Editorial Antena.

Ruhl, J.M.
1980 The Military. In A. Berry et al, eds. Politics of Compromise: Coalition Government in Colombia. New Brunswick, NJ: Transaction Books.

1978 Party System in Crisis?: An Analysis of Colombia's 1978 Elections. Inter-American Economic Affairs 32:29-45.

Ruiz Novoa, A.
1965 El gran desafío. Bogotá: Tercer Mundo.

Schoultz, L.
1972 Urbanization and Changing Voting Patterns: Colombia, 1946-1970. Political Science Quarterly 87:22-45.

Simpson, L.M.
1968 The Role of the Military in Colombian Politics. B.A. Thesis, Princeton University.

Solaún, M. and F. Cepeda
1973 Political and Legal Challenges to Foreign Direct Private Investment in Colombia. Journal of Inter-American Studies and World Affairs 15:77-101.

Stepan, A.C.
1971 The Military in Politics: Changing Patterns in Brazil. Princeton, NJ: Princeton University Press.

1973 The New Professionalism of Internal Warfare and Military Role Expansion. In A.C. Stepan, ed. Authoritarian Brazil: Origins, Policies and Future. Pp. 47-65. New Haven, CT: Yale University Press.

1978 The State and Society: Peru in Comparative Perspective. Princeton, NJ: Princeton University Press.

Studer, R.W.
1975 The Colombian Army: Political Aspects of its Role. Ph.D. dissertation, University of Southern California.

United States Arms Control and Disarmament Agency
1976 World Military Expenditures and Arms Transfers, 1966-1975.

Urrutia, M. and A. Berry
1975 La distribución del ingreso en Colombia. Medellín: Editorial Lealón.

Valencia Tovar, A.
1969 Uisheda. Bogotá: Canal Ramírez.

Van Es, J.C. and W.L. Flinn
  1973 A Note on Determinants of Satisfaction Among Urban Migrants
        in Bogotá, Colombia. Inter-American Economic Affairs
        27:15-28.

Villegas, J.
  1972 Presupuestos nacionales de ingresos y gastos, 1871-1970.
        DANE Boletín Mensual de Estadística 257-258:171-194.

Weinert, R.
  1966 Violence in Pre-Modern Societies: Rural Colombia.
        American Political Science Review 60:340-347.

Wiarda, H.J. and H.F. Kline
  1979 Latin American Politics and Development Boston, MA:
        Houghton-Mifflin.

Wilde, A.W.
  1978 Conversations Among Gentlemen: Oligarchical Democracy
        in Colombia. In J.J. Linz and A. Stepan, eds. The
        Breakdown of Democratic Regimes: Latin America.
        Pp. 28-81. Baltimore, MD: Johns Hopkins University
        Press.

13 118